Editor
Leasha Taggart

Editorial Manager
Karen J. Goldfluss, M.S. Ed.

Editor-in-Chief
Sharon Coan, M.S. Ed.

Illustrator
Ken Tunell

Cover Artist
Jessica Orlando

Art Coordinator
Denice Adorno

Creative Director
Elayne Roberts

Imaging
Alfred Lau
James Edward Grace

Product Manager
Phil Garcia

Publishers
Rachelle Cracchiolo, M.S. Ed.
Mary Dupuy Smith, M.S. Ed.

S0-AIQ-664

Brain Teasers & SQUEEZERS

Author

Mary Rosenberg

Teacher Created Materials, Inc.
6421 Industry Way
Westminster, CA 92683
www.teachercreated.com
ISBN-1-57690-653-1
©2000 Teacher Created Materials, Inc.
Reprinted, 2001
Made in U.S.A.

Table of Contents

Introduction

Brain Teasers and Squeezers is designed to develop logical thinking and reasoning and inference skills in primary-age students. The activities are divided into two main curricular areas—language arts and math. The activities in this book can be used in a variety of ways. The following are some suggestions:

Whole Class Instruction

Many of the activities can be easily done with the whole class. Make an overhead transparency of the activity and make a copy for each student in the class. Students can be called on to move pieces around (Logic Problems and More Logic Problems) or to show a solution to a problem as in Building Words. (Many of the activities can be done with just an overhead and no student copies.)

Seatwork

The activities can be assigned as seatwork or made available for students who finish an assignment early. Many of the activities can be laminated, and the student(s) can use an overhead pen to write on the laminated page. The teacher can quickly check the work, "erase" the page, and then the activity sheet is ready for the next student to use.

Advanced Students

The activities are great to use with the more advanced students in the class. Many of the activities are arranged in order from least difficult to most difficult. Make a checklist for each student in the class, and as each activity is completed, the student can place a check mark by his or her name under the specific activity.

Homework Assignments

Many of the activities are appropriate to send home as part of the weekly homework packet.

Introduction

Activity Descriptions

Word Puzzles 1–10 (pages 7–16)

The students need to write the missing letter in each circle to complete each word. After filling in each missing letter, a new word will be made from the letters written in each circle. Read the new word starting at the top and going down. Write the new word on the line. The students complete a short activity using the "mystery word" (new word).

What's the Rule? (pages 17–20)

The students read the words already listed (words #1–6) and discover the "rule," or what the six words have in common. The students then read the words in the word bank and select the words that meet the rule. The selected words are written on lines 7–12. The students then write the rule and complete a short activity related to the rule.

Compound Riddles (pages 21–23)

Ten compound words on a common topic are separated into the beginnings (first part of the word) and endings (second part of the word). The students read each clue and figure out which compound word answers each riddle. The students write the compound word on the lines. (Picture clues for each compound word are provided as well as lines for each letter in the compound word.)

Building Words (pages 24–30)

Anagrams are words that are made by rearranging the letters to form another word. The activities on these pages provide a "twist" to the traditional anagram by directing students to first rearrange the letters to make a new word and then having them subtract one letter each time a new word is made. For each word, several word choices are possible.

Logic Problems (pages 31–42)

The students arrange different items on logic mats according to a variety of clues read by the teacher. The students also complete a sentence about the logic mat or make up their own logic problems.

Introduction

Activity Descriptions *(cont.)*

More Logic Problems—Brain Squeezers (pages 43–46)

The students need to arrange nine of the number squares so that the numbers going across and down all equal a specific number. (**Note:** Not all of the number squares will be used.)

Twelve-Picture Logic (pages 47–52)

The students listen to (or read) clues and place an **X** on the pictures that do not meet the clue. After listening to and following all of the clues, there should be only one picture left. The students write the number of the remaining picture and a new clue to fit that picture.

Logic Grids (pages 53–60)

The students read each clue. If the answer is **yes**, the students make an **X** in the box. If the answer is **no**, the students make an **O** in the box.

Camp Fish 'n Fun

1. Reba does not like to go canoeing or fishing. Place **O's** in the columns by Reba's name under canoeing and fishing. There is only one activity left for Reba and that is "marshmallows." Place an **X** in the marshmallow column by Reba's name. Since Reba likes roasting marshmallows, that means Dean and Jake don't like roasting marshmallows. Make an **O** by Dean and Jake's names under the marshmallow column.

	🎣	🛶	〰️
Dean	X	O	O
Jake	O	X	O
Reba	O	O	X

2. Dean likes to go fishing. (Place an **X** in the fishing column by Dean's name. Place an **O** in the canoeing column. Based on the clues, there is only one empty activity left, and that is canoeing. Place an **X** in the canoeing column by Jake's name.)

Introduction

Activity Descriptions *(cont.)*

Adding Games (pages 61–65)

Students use crayons to color in 2–4 squares that add up to the specified number. The squares must touch on the sides—not just at the corners.

For one player: Use several different colors of crayons to color in the numbers that equal the specified number.

For example, if adding to 6, a student might use a red crayon to color in the squares with the numbers 1, 2, and 3. All 3 squares will be colored red. For the next set of numbers, the student will use a different color of crayon.

For two players: Each player will choose his or her favorite color of crayon. Taking turns, each player colors in the squares needed to reach a specific number.

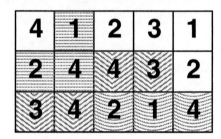

One player—The different shadings represent different colors of crayons. (The students would use different colors of crayons to color in the numbers instead of shading in the used numbers.)

Two players—Each player has his own kind of shading. (The students would use crayons to color in the numbers instead of shading.)

Money Problems (pages 66–70)

Students cut out the money and arrange the coins to make different combinations for the given amounts of money. A page of paper coins is provided to use as manipulatives.

Shape Recognition (pages 71–73)

Students count the number of shapes in each picture, write the numbers on the line, and color the picture. Students can also color each shape a different color to help them keep track (colors will overlap).

Numbers and Operations (pages 74 and 75)

Students fill in the correct sign (+, –, or =) to make each problem correct.

Manipulatives (pages 76 and 77)

These pages may be reproduced as needed, cut out by students, and used to help with the math or language arts activities.

Word Puzzle #1

Look at each picture. Read the word that goes with each picture. Write the missing letter in the circle. After all of the circles have been filled in, find the mystery word.

1.    c a ◯

2.    n ◯ t

3.   m a ◯

4.   ◯ a t

5.    ◯ c e

6.    ◯ e a f

What is the mystery word? ___ ___ ___ ___ ___ ___

Draw a picture of the mystery word.

Word Puzzle #2

Look at each picture. Read the word that goes with each picture. Write the missing letter in the circle. After all of the circles have been filled in, find the mystery word.

1. ◯ e n t

2. n ◯ s t

3. p ◯ d d l e

4. ◯ a n o e

5. ◯ a m b u r g e r

6. ◯ g g

7. c ◯ a b

What is the mystery word? ___ ___ ___ ___ ___ ___ ___

Draw a picture of the mystery word.

Word Puzzle #3

Look at each picture. Read the word that goes with each picture. Write the missing letter in the circle. After all of the circles have been filled in, find the mystery word.

1.   s h ◯ l l

2.    s c a ◯ e c r o w

3.    f l ◯ g

4.   ◯ e w

5.   j ◯ t

6.   b e a ◯

What is the mystery word? ___ ___ ___ ___ ___ ___

Draw a picture of the mystery word.

Word Puzzle #4

Look at each picture. Read the word that goes with each picture. Write the missing letter in the circle. After all of the circles have been filled in, find the mystery word.

1.  ◯ e e r

2.  b ◯ d

3.  b a ◯ k e t

4.  ◯ i t e

What is the mystery word? ___ ___ ___ ___

Draw a picture of the mystery word.

Use the mystery word in a sentence.

_____

_____

_____

Word Puzzle #5

Look at each picture. Read the word that goes with each picture. Write the missing letter in the circle. After all of the circles have been filled in, find the mystery word.

1. ◯ l o w n

2.  ◯ a t

3.  b ◯ n d

4.  b ◯ k e

5. s t a ◯

What is the mystery word? ___ ___ ___ ___ ___

Draw a picture of the mystery word.

Use the mystery word in a sentence.

_____

_____

_____

Word Puzzle #6

Look at each picture. Read the word that goes with each picture. Write the missing letter in the circle. After all of the circles have been filled in, find the mystery word.

1.  d i ◯ h

2.  ◯ l o u d

3.   ◯ e n

4.  ◯ c t o p u s

5.  b o ◯ k

6.  ◯ a m p

What is the mystery word? ___ ___ ___ ___ ___ ___

Draw a picture of the mystery word.

Use the mystery word in a sentence.

_____

- -

_____

- -

_____

Word Puzzle #7

Look at each picture. Read the word that goes with each picture. Write the missing letter in the circle. After all of the circles have been filled in, find the mystery word.

 1.   ◯ h a i r

2.    o ◯ a n g e

3.    c ◯ t

4. 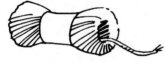   ◯ a r n

5.   m ◯ o n

6.   s u ◯

What is the mystery word? ___ ___ ___ ___ ___ ___

Draw a picture of the mystery word.

Use the mystery word in a sentence.

_____

- -
_____
_____
- -
_____

Word Puzzle #8

Look at each picture. Read the word that goes with each picture. Write the missing letter in the circle. After all of the circles have been filled in, find the mystery word.

1. 〇 h o e

2. 〇 r e e

3. 〇 m b r e l l a

4. 〇 i m e

5. f 〇 n c e

6. 〇 i c k e l

7.  m a 〇

What is the mystery word? ___ ___ ___ ___ ___ ___

Use the mystery word in a sentence.

_____

_____

_____

Word Puzzle #9

Look at each picture. Read the word that goes with each picture. Write the missing letter in the circle. After all of the circles have been filled in, find the mystery word.

1.   a p p ◯ e

2.   m ◯ l k

3.   ◯ a c o n

4.    b ◯ e a d

5.    w ◯ f f l e

6.    g ◯ a p e s

7.    h a ◯

What is the mystery word? ___ ___ ___ ___ ___ ___ ___

Use the mystery word in a sentence.

_____

- -

_____

- -

_____

Word Puzzle #10

Look at each picture. Read the word that goes with each picture. Write the missing letter in the circle. After all of the circles have been filled in, find the mystery word.

1. ◯ r i c k e t

2. m ◯ t h

3.  w o r ◯

4.  g r a s s h o ◯ p e r

5.  l a d y b ◯ g

6.  a n ◯

7.  b ◯ e

8.  b u t t e ◯ f l y

What is the mystery word? ___ ___ ___ ___ ___ ___ ___ ___

Use the mystery word in a sentence.

_____

_____

_____

What's the Rule?

Look at the words on the list below. What do they all have in common? Choose words from the Word Bank that meet the rule. Write the words from the Word Bank on the lines.

Word Bank

orange	house	green
desk	purple	phone
brown	yellow	red
flower	table	tape

1. pink
2. gray
3. blue
4. black
5. white
6. gold

7. _____
8. _____
9. _____
10. _____
11. _____
12. _____

What is the rule? _____

_____
_____

_____

What is your favorite color? _____

_____

What's the Rule?

Look at the words on the list below. What do they all have in common? Choose words from the Word Bank that meet the rule. Write the words from the Word Bank on the lines.

Word Bank

jr.	CA	min.
California	captain	junior
capt.	in.	inch
foot	minute	ft.

1. Dr.

2. Ms.

3. Mrs.

4. Ave.

5. St.

6. bldg.

7. _____

8. _____

9. _____

10. _____

11. _____

12. _____

What is the rule?
_____
- -
_____
_____
- -
_____

Can you think of any other words that would fit the rule?
- -
_____

What's the Rule?

Look at the words on the list below. What do they all have in common?
Choose words from the Word Bank that meet the rule. Write the words
from the Word Bank on the lines.

Word Bank

checkers	volleyball	Monopoly®
football	chess	soccer
baseball	Yahtzee®	Memory®
Uno®	rugby	tennis

1. crazy eights
2. Connect Four®
3. Sorry®
4. pick-up-sticks
5. Twister®
6. Boggle®

7. _____
8. _____
9. _____
10. _____
11. _____
12. _____

What is the rule?

_____
_____
_____
_____

Write the name of the game you like to play that fits the rule.

_____

What's the Rule?

Look at the words on the list below. What do they all have in common? Choose words from the Word Bank that meet the rule. Write the words from the Word Bank on the lines.

Word Bank

Ben	October	January
May	Paula	Marla
Carla	April	Donald
September	Zachary	July

1. February
2. December
3. June
4. August
5. November
6. March

7. _____
8. _____
9. _____
10. _____
11. _____
12. _____

What is the rule?

_____

_____
_____

_____

Use one of the words in a sentence.

_____

_____

Compound Riddles

Ten compound words have been separated into two parts: the beginning part of the compound word and the ending part of the compound word. Put the compound words back together again by answering each riddle. Write the completed compound words on the lines.

Beginnings		Endings	
basket	over	ball	color
book	note	board	ground
chalk	video	book	head
class	play	case	mate
hop	water	tape	scotch

1. I am used to record memories. __ __ __ __ __ + __ __ __ __

2. I can be used to make a pretty picture.

   __ __ __ __ __ + __ __ __ __ __

3. I can be used to make writing and pictures really big.

   __ __ __ __ + __ __ __ __

4. People can write on me. __ __ __ __ __ + __ __ __ __ __

5. I can be found in the library. __ __ __ __ + __ __ __ __

6. I am thrown through a hoop. __ __ __ __ __ __ + __ __ __ __

7. People hop in squares to play me. __ __ __ + __ __ __ __ __ __

8. I have lots of papers with lines. __ __ __ __ + __ __ __ __

9. I am another student at school. __ __ __ __ __ __ + __ __ __ __

10. This is where you go at recess. __ __ __ __ __ + __ __ __ __ __ __

Compound Riddles

Ten compound words have been separated into two parts: the beginning part of the compound word and the ending part of the compound word. Put the compound words back together again by answering each riddle. Write the completed compound words on the lines.

Beginnings		Endings	
cup	pea	apple	dog
grape	pine	berry	fruit
hot	pop	cake	melon
milk	straw	cake	nut
pan	water	corn	shake

1. I am a plump red fruit. __ __ __ __ __ + __ __ __ __ __

2. I am shaken and have ice cream in me.

   __ __ __ __ + __ __ __ __ __

3. I am a type of nut. __ __ __ + __ __ __

4. I am eaten for breakfast. __ __ __ + __ __ __ __

5. I am eaten at birthday parties. __ __ __ + __ __ __ __

6. I am a big fruit with lots of black seeds.

   __ __ __ __ __ + __ __ __ __ __

7. I am eaten at baseball games. __ __ __ + __ __ __

8. I make a popping noise when I am cooked.

   __ __ __ + __ __ __ __

9. I am yellow or pink inside and grow on a tree.

   __ __ __ __ __ + __ __ __ __ __

10. I am neither green nor red. __ __ __ __ + __ __ __ __ __

Compound Riddles

Ten compound words have been separated into two parts: the beginning part of the compound word and the ending part of the compound word. Put the compound words back together again by answering each riddle. Write the completed compound words on the lines.

Beginnings		Endings	
bull	humming	bird	fly
butter	jelly	bug	head
gold	lady	dog	hopper
grass	road	fish	horse
hammer	sea	fish	runner

1. I like to drink nectar. __ __ __ __ __ __ __ + __ __ __ __

2. I can be a boy even though I have a girl's name.

   __ __ __ __ + __ __ __

3. I have beautiful wings. __ __ __ __ __ __ + __ __ __

4. I am a small green insect.

   __ __ __ __ __ + __ __ __ __ __ __

5. I usually live in a tank or pond. __ __ __ __ + __ __ __ __

6. I am a type of shark. __ __ __ __ __ __ + __ __ __ __

7. I live in the ocean, but I don't give rides.

   __ __ __ + __ __ __ __ __

8. I am in a lot of cartoons. __ __ __ __ + __ __ __ __ __ __

9. Don't put me on a peanut butter sandwich!

   __ __ __ __ __ + __ __ __ __

10. I'm a canine with a large square jaw. __ __ __ __ __ + __ __ __

Building Words

Look at the first word. Take away one letter and rearrange the remaining letters to make a new word. Continue taking away one letter and making a new word until the last word is a two-letter word.

Example: star

_r_ _a_ _t_

_a_ _t_

1. mate

___ ___ ___

___ ___

2. sand

___ ___ ___

___ ___

3. stop

___ ___ ___

___ ___

4. lamp

___ ___ ___

___ ___

5. ears

___ ___ ___

___ ___

6. soap

___ ___ ___

___ ___

7. taps

___ ___ ___

___ ___

Mind Challenge!

How many words can you make using the letters in *elevator?* Write the words on a separate piece of paper.

Building Words

Look at the first word. Take away one letter and rearrange the remaining letters to make a new word. Continue taking away one letter and making a new word until the last word is a two-letter word.

Example: taxi

t a x

a x

1. four

___ ___ ___

___ ___

2. time

___ ___ ___

___ ___

3. barn

___ ___ ___

___ ___

4. post

___ ___ ___

___ ___

5. mail

___ ___ ___

___ ___

6. king

___ ___ ___

___ ___

7. ties

___ ___ ___

___ ___

Mind Challenge!

How many words can you make using the letters in *dinosaur?* Write the words on a separate piece of paper.

Building Words

Look at the first word. Take away one letter and rearrange the remaining letters to make a new word. Continue taking away one letter and making a new word until the last word is a two-letter word.

Example: game	1. gift	2. pink
g e m	__ __ __	__ __ __
m e	__ __	__ __

3. your	4. mask	5. tear
__ __ __	__ __ __	__ __ __
__ __	__ __	__ __

6. fire	7. shoe	**Mind Challenge!**
		How many words can you make using the letters in *breakfast?* Write the words on a separate piece of paper.
__ __ __	__ __ __	
__ __	__ __	

Building Words

Look at the first word. Take away one letter and rearrange the remaining letters to make a new word. Continue taking away one letter and making a new word until the last word is a two-letter word.

Example: ocean

c o n e

o n e

o n

1. spine

___ ___ ___ ___

___ ___ ___

___ ___

2. stamp

___ ___ ___ ___

___ ___ ___

___ ___

3. heart

___ ___ ___ ___

___ ___ ___

___ ___

4. plate

___ ___ ___ ___

___ ___ ___

___ ___

5. watch

___ ___ ___ ___

___ ___ ___

___ ___

6. stick

___ ___ ___ ___

___ ___ ___

___ ___

7. light

___ ___ ___ ___

___ ___ ___

___ ___

Mind Challenge!

How many words can you make using the letters in *president?* Write the words on a separate piece of paper.

Building Words

Look at the first word. Take away one letter and rearrange the remaining letters to make a new word. Continue taking away one letter and making a new word until the last word is a two-letter word.

Example: ghost

h o s t

h o t

t o

1. shape

_ _ _ _

_ _ _

_ _

2. clasp

_ _ _ _

_ _ _

_ _

3. video

_ _ _ _

_ _ _

_ _

4. cover

_ _ _ _

_ _ _

_ _

5. pants

_ _ _ _

_ _ _

_ _

6. shirt

_ _ _ _

_ _ _

_ _

7. drink

_ _ _ _

_ _ _

_ _

Mind Challenge!

How many words can you make using the letters in *principal?* Write the words on a separate piece of paper.

Building Words

Look at the first word. Take away one letter and rearrange the remaining letters to make a new word. Continue taking away one letter and making a new word until the last word is a two-letter word.

Example: swing

w i n g

w i n

i n

1. straw

___ ___ ___ ___

___ ___ ___

___ ___

2. plant

___ ___ ___ ___

___ ___ ___

___ ___

3. phone

___ ___ ___ ___

___ ___ ___

___ ___

4. horse

___ ___ ___ ___

___ ___ ___

___ ___

5. stink

___ ___ ___ ___

___ ___ ___

___ ___

6. sweep

___ ___ ___ ___

___ ___ ___

___ ___

7. plate

___ ___ ___ ___

___ ___ ___

___ ___

Mind Challenge!

How many words can you make using the letters in *teacher?* Write the words on a separate piece of paper.

Building Words

Look at the first word. Take away one letter and rearrange the remaining letters to make a new word. Continue taking away one letter and making a new word until the last word is a two-letter word.

Example: flower

l o w e r

w o r e

r o w

o r

1. travel

_ _ _ _ _

_ _ _ _

_ _ _

_ _

2. dinner

_ _ _ _ _

_ _ _ _

_ _ _

_ _

3. please

_ _ _ _ _

_ _ _ _

_ _ _

_ _

4. plates

_ _ _ _ _

_ _ _ _

_ _ _

_ _

5. staple

_ _ _ _ _

_ _ _ _

_ _ _

_ _

6. camera

_ _ _ _ _

_ _ _ _

_ _ _

_ _

7. thinks

_ _ _ _ _

_ _ _ _

_ _ _

_ _

Mind Challenge!

How many words can you make using the letters in *friend?* Write the words on a separate piece of paper.

Back to School

Use the logic problems mat and the picture squares on page 32 to solve these logic problems.

①

The eraser is first.

The pencil is second.

The crayons are third.

②

The eraser is first.

The crayons are second.

The pencil is third.

③

The pencil is first.

The crayons are second.

The eraser is third.

④

The pencil is first.

The eraser is second.

The crayons are third.

⑤

The crayons are third.

The pencil is second.

The eraser is first.

⑥

The crayons are first.

The eraser is second.

The pencil is third.

⑦

The pencil is first.

The crayons are last.

The eraser is in between the pencil and the crayons.

⑧

The crayons are first.

The eraser is last.

The pencil is in between the crayons and the eraser.

⑨

The crayons are first.

The eraser is after the crayons.

The pencil is after the eraser.

⑩

The eraser is last.

The crayons are before the eraser.

The pencil is before the crayons.

Back to School

Cut out the squares at the bottom of the page. Use them in the logic mat boxes below to help you solve the problems on page 31.

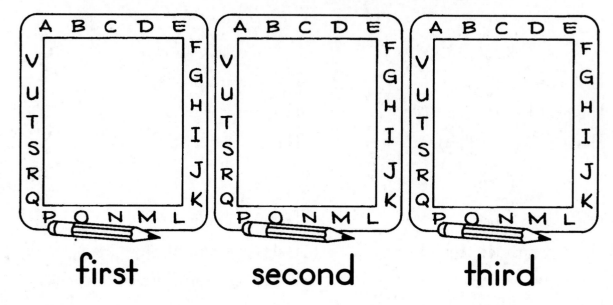

first   second   third

My favorite school supply is

Sun, Moon, and Stars

Use the logic problems mat and the picture squares on page 34 to solve these logic problems.

1

The stars are first.

The sun is second.

The moon is third.

2

The moon is first.

The sun is second.

The stars are third.

3

The sun is first.

The stars are second.

The moon is third.

4

The moon is first.

The stars are second.

The sun is third.

5

The sun is first.

The moon is second.

The stars are third.

6

The stars are first.

The moon is second.

The sun is third.

7

The sun is first.

The stars are next.

The moon is after the stars.

8

The stars are first.

The moon is last.

The sun is after the stars and before the moon.

9

The sun is last.

The stars are before the sun.

The moon is before the stars.

10

The sun is first.

The stars are last.

The moon is after the sun and before the stars.

Sun, Moon, and Stars

Cut out the squares at the bottom of the page. Use them in the logic mat boxes below to help you solve the problems on page 33.

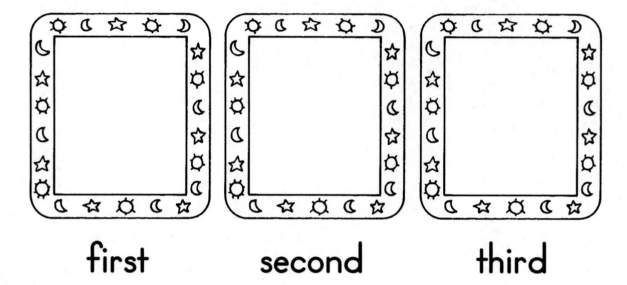

first   second   third

My favorite shape is the

A Sea Full of Life

Use the logic problems mat and the picture squares on page 36 to solve these logic problems.

1

The crab is first.
The octopus is second.
The fish is third.
The oyster is last.

2

The octopus is first.
The fish comes after the octopus.
The oyster is last.
The crab is in between the fish and the oyster.

3

The fish is first.
The oyster is third.
The crab is in between the fish and the oyster.
The octopus is after the oyster.

4

The crab is last.
The octopus is second.
The oyster is before the octopus.
The fish is before the crab.

5

The fish is first.
The octopus is third.
The crab is before the octopus.
The oyster is after the octopus.

6

The fish is last.
The oyster is before the fish.
The octopus is not second.
The crab is after the octopus.

7

The crab is first.
The octopus is last.
The fish is before the octopus.
The oyster is before the fish.

8

The crab is last.
The fish is two places before the crab.
The octopus is not first.
The oyster is before the fish.

9

The oyster is third.
The octopus is after the oyster.
The fish is before the oyster.
The crab is before the fish.

10

The fish is first.
The crab is two places after the fish.
The oyster is last.
The octopus is before the crab and after the fish.

A Sea Full of Life

Cut out the squares at the bottom of the page. Use them in the logic mat boxes below to help you solve the problems on page 35.

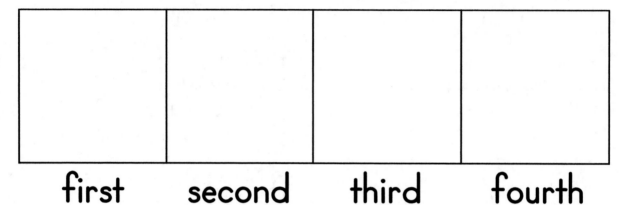

first	second	third	fourth

Write your own logic problem.

1. The _____ is first.

2. The _____ is second.

3. The _____ is third.

4. The _____ is fourth.

Let's Go to the Zoo

Use the logic problems mat and the picture squares on page 38 to help you solve these logic problems.

The hippo is first.
The giraffe is second.
The panda is third.
The kangaroo is last.

The kangaroo is first.
The hippo is second.
The giraffe is third.
The panda is last.

The giraffe is first.
The kangaroo is third.
The hippo is not last.
The panda is after the kangaroo.

The panda is first.
The kangaroo is last.
The hippo is not third.
The giraffe is before the kangaroo.

The panda is third.
The giraffe is after the panda.
The kangaroo is before the panda.
The hippo is before the kangaroo.

The kangaroo is second.
The panda is third.
The giraffe is after the panda.
The hippo is before the kangaroo.

The giraffe is last.
The kangaroo is first.
The panda is after the kangaroo.
The hippo is before the giraffe.

The giraffe is second.
The panda is before the giraffe.
The kangaroo is last.
The hippo is after the giraffe.

The hippo is first.
The panda is last.
The giraffe is before the panda.
The kangaroo is before the giraffe.

The kangaroo is first.
The panda is third.
The giraffe is last.
The hippo is before the panda.

Let's Go to the Zoo

Cut out the squares at the bottom of the page. Use them in the logic mat boxes below to help you solve the problems on page 37.

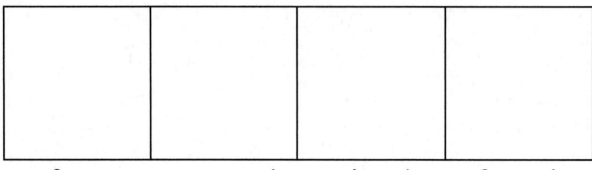

first	second	third	fourth

Write your own logic problem.

1. _____

2. _____

3. _____

4. _____

Now We're Cooking!

Use the logic problems mat and the picture squares on page 42 to solve these logic problems.

①

The rolling pin is first.
The recipe card is second.
The spoon is third.
The mixing bowl is fourth.
The milk is fifth.

②

The spoon is first.
The milk is third.
The recipe card is last.
The mixing bowl is after the spoon.
The rolling pin is after the milk.

③

The rolling pin is last.
The mixing bowl is first.
The spoon is third.
The milk is three places after the mixing bowl.
The recipe card is after the mixing bowl.

④

The spoon is fourth.
The rolling pin is after the spoon.
The mixing bowl is before the spoon.
The milk is first.
The recipe card is after the milk.

⑤

The rolling pin is second.
The milk is before the rolling pin.
The recipe card is after the rolling pin.
The mixing bowl is last.
The spoon is three places after the milk.

⑥

The spoon is third.
The mixing bowl is after the spoon.
The rolling pin is before the spoon.
The recipe card is not last.
The milk is not first.

⑦

The recipe card is second.
The milk is before the recipe card.
The rolling pin is last.
The mixing bowl is not third.
The spoon is before the mixing bowl.

⑧

The mixing bowl is last.
The rolling pin is first.
The milk is after the rolling pin.
The spoon is before the mixing bowl.
The recipe card is before the spoon.

⑨

The mixing bowl is first.
The recipe card is fourth.
The spoon is last.
The rolling pin is in the middle.
The milk is after the mixing bowl.

⑩

The spoon is first.
The rolling pin is last.
The mixing bowl is in the middle.
The milk is after the mixing bowl.
The recipe card is after the spoon.

Now We're Cooking!

Cut out the squares at the bottom of the page. Use them in the logic mat boxes below to help you solve the problems on page 39.

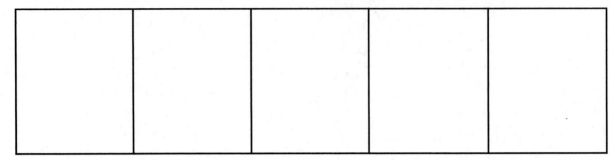

| first | second | third | fourth | fifth |

Write your own logic problem.

1. _____

2. _____

3. _____

4. _____

5. _____

Are We There Yet?

Use the logic problems mat and the picture squares on page 42 to solve these logic problems.

(1)

The sailboat is first.
The plane is last.
The bus is in the middle.
The car is after the bus.
The train is before the bus.

(2)

The car is first.
The train is last.
The bus is before the train.
The sailboat is second.
The plane is in the middle.

(3)

The car is third.
The sailboat is two places after the car.
The plane is two places before the car.
The train is second.
The bus is next to last.

(4)

The bus is second.
The train is before the bus.
The sailboat is last.
The car is third.
The plane is before the sailboat.

(5)

The plane is first.
The bus is two places after the plane.
The car is in between the plane and the bus.
The train is last.
The sailboat is after the bus.

(6)

The train is last.
The sailboat is before the train.
The bus is two places before the sailboat.
The car is before the sailboat.
The plane is before the bus.

(7)

The car is fourth.
The train is three places before the car.
The sailboat is after the train.
The bus is not last.
The plane is after the car.

(8)

The sailboat is fourth.
The train is after the sailboat.
The car is first.
The plane is not third.
The bus is after the plane.

(9)

The plane is fourth.
The train is first.
The bus is after the plane.
The sailboat is not second.
The car is before the sailboat.

(10)

The sailboat is fourth.
The train is after the sailboat.
The plane is before the sailboat.
The bus is not first.
The car is first.

Are We There Yet?

Cut out the squares at the bottom of the page. Use them in the logic mat boxes below to help you solve the problems on page 41.

first   **second**   **third**   **fourth**   **fifth**

Write your own logic problem.

1. _____

2. _____

3. _____

4. _____

5. _____

Brain Squeezer to 12

Cut out the numbers below. Place a number in each square so that the numbers add up to 12 going across and down. When the numbers have been arranged correctly, glue the numbers in the squares.

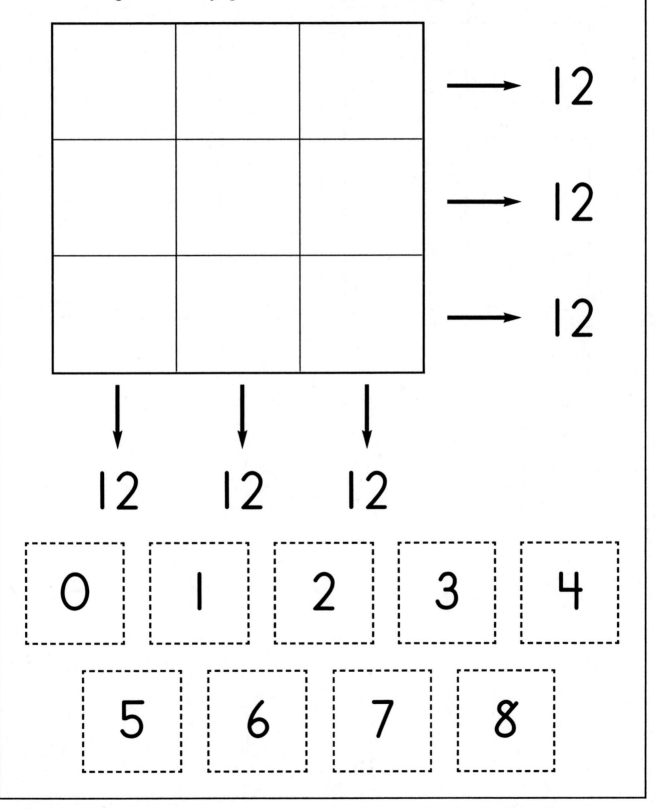

Brain Squeezer to 15

Cut out the numbers below. Place a number in each square so that the numbers add up to 15 going across and down. When the numbers have been arranged correctly, glue the numbers in the squares.

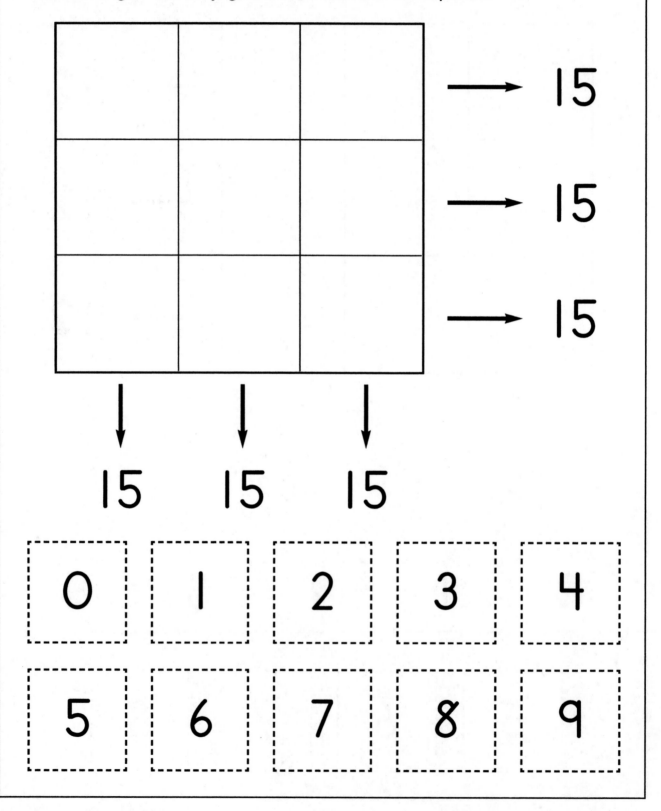

Brain Squeezer to 18

Cut out the numbers below. Place a number in each square so that the numbers add up to 18 going across and down. When the numbers have been arranged correctly, glue the numbers in the squares.

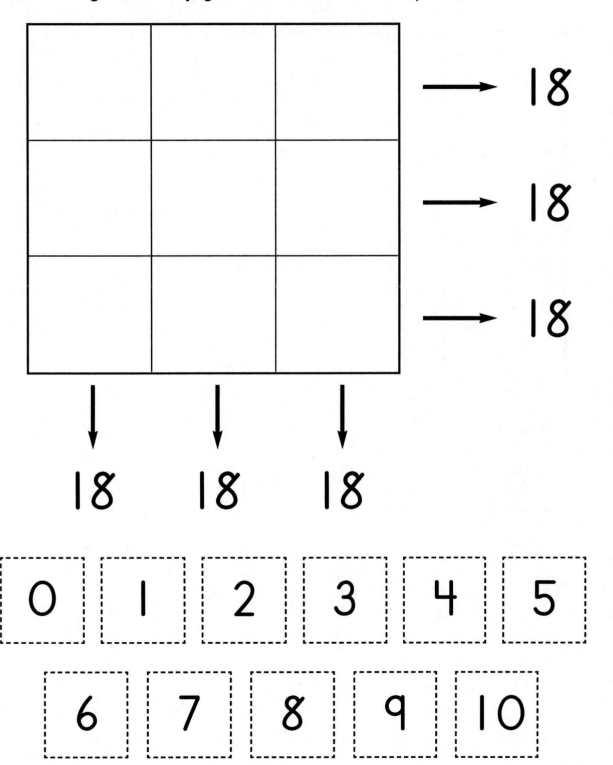

Brain Squeezer to 21

Cut out the numbers below. Place a number in each square so that the numbers add up to 21 going across and down. When the numbers have been arranged correctly, glue the numbers in the squares.

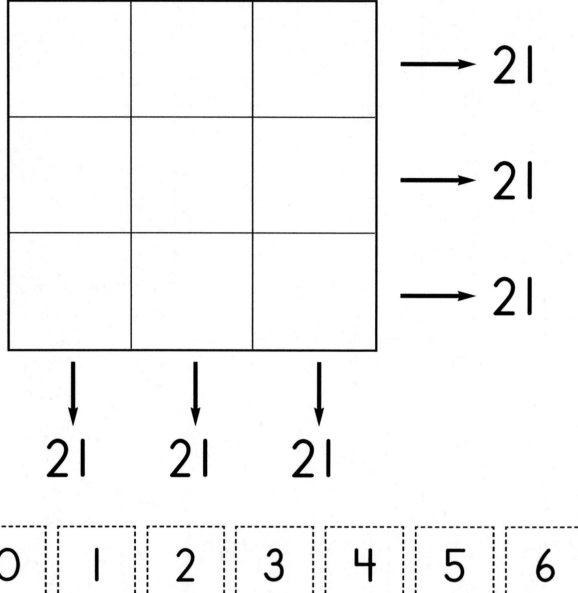

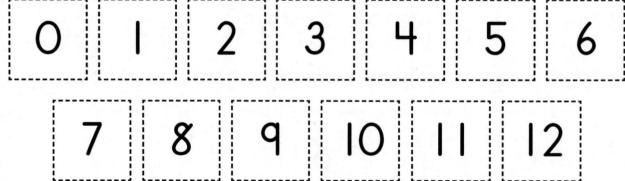

Eat Your Fruits and Vegetables

Read each clue. Put an **X** on the picture(s) that do not fit each clue.
After answering all of the clues, there will be one picture left.

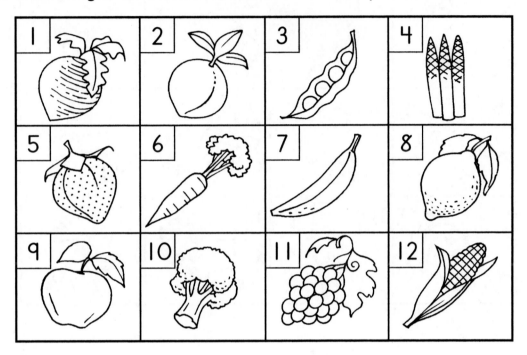

Clues:

1. I do not have a green leaf.
2. I am not a green fruit or vegetable.
3. I grow on plants.

Which one am I? _____

_____

Write a clue that would fit this fruit or vegetable.

_____

_____

_____

Here, Kitty, Kitty

Read each clue. Put an **X** on the picture(s) that do not fit each clue.
After answering all of the clues, there will be one picture left.

Clues:

1. I am a house cat.

2. I have stripes.

3. I am wearing a collar.

Which cat am I? --

Write a clue that would fit this cat.

Going Buggy!

Read each clue. Put an **X** on the picture(s) that do not fit each clue. After answering all of the clues, there will be one picture left.

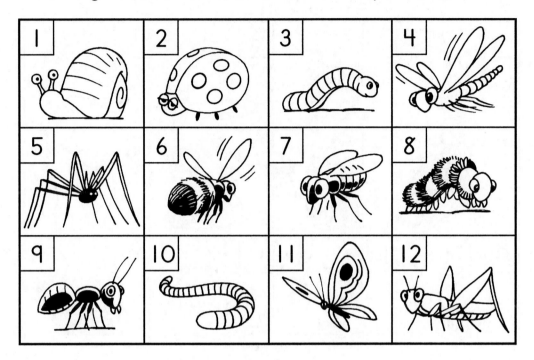

Clues:

1. I have legs that you can see.

2. I have a hard shell on my body.

3. I can fly and have spots on my body.

Which bug am I? _____

_____

Write a clue that would fit this bug. _____

_____

Which Animal Am I?

Read each clue. Put an **X** on the picture(s) that do not fit each clue. After answering all of the clues, there will be one picture left.

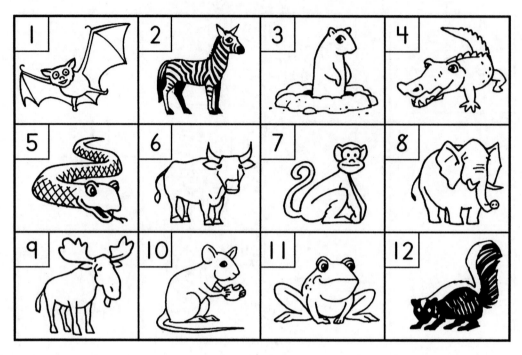

Clues:

1. I do not have horns, tusks, or hooves.

2. I am standing on four legs.

3. I am a mammal. (A mammal is an animal that is born alive. It does not hatch from an egg.)

Which animal am I? --

Write a clue that would fit this animal.

Which Puppy Is It?

Read each clue. Put an **X** on the picture(s) that do not fit each clue. After answering all of the clues, there will be one picture left.

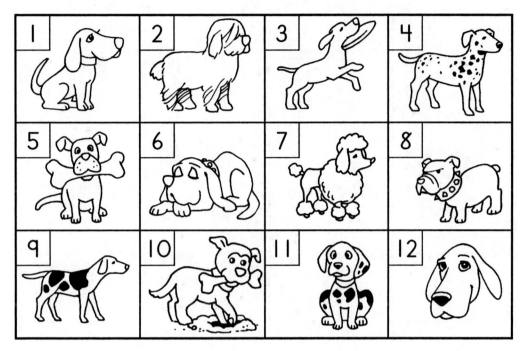

Clues:

1. I do not have spots.
2. I am not wearing a dog collar.
3. I have a body.
4. I have four paws on the ground.
5. I do not have a bone.
6. I cannot see.

Which puppy am I? ------------------------------------

Write a clue that would fit this puppy.

Which Flag Am I?

Read each clue. Put an **X** on the picture(s) that do not fit each clue. After answering all of the clues, there will be one picture left.

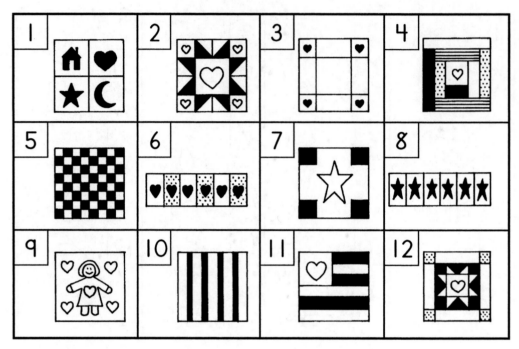

Clues:

1. I do not have a square in each corner.
2. My flag is square in shape. (going around the outside of the flag)
3. I do not have any stars.
4. I have only one heart.
5. I do not have any dots.

Which flag am I? _____

_____

Write a clue that would fit this flag.

_____

Spring Planting

Read each clue. If the answer is *yes,* make an **X** in the box. If the answer is *no,* make an **O** in the box.

1. Gus planted grapes in his garden.

2. Vincent planted watermelon seeds in his garden.

Next to each fruit, write the name of the boy who planted it in his garden.

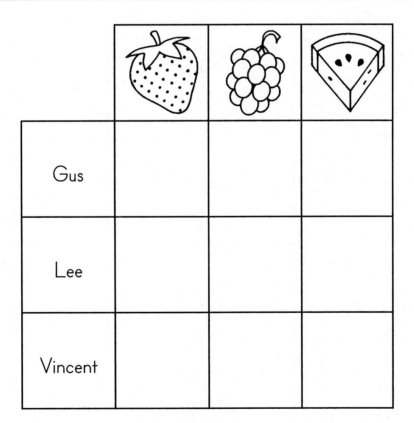

Bonus: Which two fruit names are also compound words?

_____

_____

Fish 'n Fun

Read each clue. If the answer is *yes,* make an **X** in the box. If the answer is *no,* make an **O** in the box.

1. Reba does not like to go canoeing or fishing.

2. Dean likes to go fishing.

Next to each camping activity, write the name of the person who enjoys it.

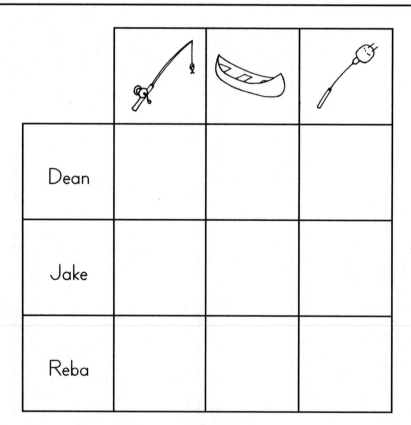

Bonus: Which person caught the most fish?

Let's Play Ball!

Read each clue. If the answer is *yes*, make an **X** in the box. If the answer is *no*, make an **O** in the box.

1. Ann plays first base for the Sharks.

2. Dan does not play first base for the Tigers.

Next to each baseball team, write the player's name.

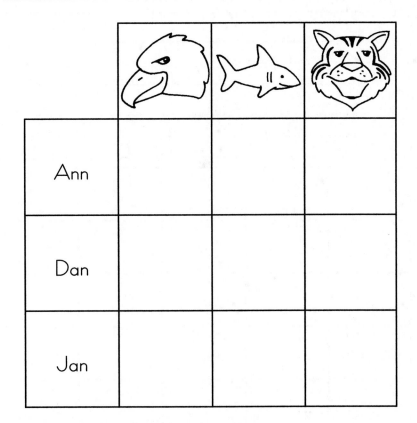

Bonus: Who plays first base for the Tigers?

_____

_____

Birthdays! Birthdays! Birthdays!

Read each clue. If the answer is *yes,* make an **X** in the box. If the answer is *no,* make an **O** in the box.

1. Patrick's birthday is in August.
2. Cara's birthday is not in January.
3. Freddy's birthday is not in January.
4. Cara's birthday is in March.

Next to each month, write the birthday person's name.

Jan. _____

Mar. _____

Aug. _____

Nov. _____

	Jan.	Mar.	Aug.	Nov.
Cara				
Latoya				
Freddy				
Patrick				

Bonus: How many months are not mentioned in this logic problem?

_____

Favorite Shoes

Read each clue. If the answer is *yes,* make an **X** in the box. If the answer is *no,* make an **O** in the box.

1. Thomas wears cowboy boots.
2. Neither Ralph nor Maureen has tennis shoes.
3. Ralph never wears sandals.

Next to each kind of shoe, write the wearer's name.

	🥾	👢	👡	👟
Emma				
Maureen				
Ralph				
Thomas				

Bonus: Which shoes usually do not have laces?

Pony Rides

Read each clue. If the answer is *yes,* make an **X** in the box. If the answer is *no,* make an **O** in the box.

1. Sean's horse is gray.
2. Chelsea's white horse's name is Bubbles.
3. Howie's horse's name is Spot.

Next to each horse, write the name of the person who rode the horse and the horse's color. (Each horse is a different color.)

	Rider	Color
Bubbles	_____	_____
Ranger	_____	_____
Spot	_____	_____

	Bubbles	Ranger	Spot	black	gray	white
Chelsea						
Howie						
Sean						

Bonus: How do you think the horse named Spot got his name?

_____

_____

Plenty of Pie

Read each clue. If the answer is *yes*, make an **X** in the box. If the answer is *no*, make an **O** in the box.

1. Belle ate 6 pieces of pie.
2. Cedric loves strawberry pie.
3. Noreen likes blueberry pie best.
4. Cedric did not eat 5 pieces of pie.

Next to each kind of pie, write and the name of the person who ate the pie and the number of pieces eaten.

	Pie Eater	Pieces
blueberry		
cherry		
strawberry		

	blueberry	cherry	strawberry	5 pieces	6 pieces	7 pieces
Belle						
Cedric						
Noreen						

Bonus: Who ate the most pieces of pie?

_____

_____

Friendly Frogs

Read each clue. If the answer is *yes*, make an **X** in the box. If the answer is *no*, make an **O** in the box.

1. Gilbert has the fewest number of frogs.
2. Chris has the orange frogs.
3. Tonya has the most frogs.
4. Gilbert does not like blue frogs.

Next to each color of frog, write and the name of the frogs' owner and the number of frogs.

	Frogs' Owner	Number
blue		
green		
orange		

	5	10	15	blue	green	orange
Chris						
Gilbert						
Tanya						

Bonus: The number of each kind of frog makes a pattern. What is the pattern?

Add to 6

1	2	2	1	1	2	2	1	2	2
2	2	1	1	1	2	2	2	2	1
1	2	1	1	2	2	1	1	1	2
1	2	1	2	2	2	1	2	1	2
1	2	2	2	1	2	1	1	1	2
2	2	1	2	1	1	2	2	2	1
2	1	1	2	1	2	1	2	2	1
2	1	2	1	1	2	1	1	1	1
2	1	2	1	2	2	1	2	2	1
1	2	2	1	2	1	2	1	1	2

Add to 7

3	2	3	4	1	2	4	3	2	2
3	2	3	1	1	2	2	3	2	1
1	2	1	3	2	4	1	4	3	2
1	2	4	2	3	2	1	2	3	4
1	2	4	4	1	2	1	4	3	4
2	3	4	3	4	3	2	3	4	3
4	1	3	2	4	2	1	3	2	1
4	1	2	3	1	4	1	1	1	4
2	4	4	3	2	4	3	2	3	4
3	4	2	1	4	1	2	3	4	4

Add to 8

Teacher Directions: See page 6.

3	2	3	1	1	2	2	3	2	2
3	2	3	1	1	2	2	3	2	1
1	2	1	3	2	3	1	1	3	2
1	2	1	2	3	2	1	2	3	2
1	2	2	3	1	2	1	1	3	2
2	3	3	3	1	3	2	3	2	3
3	1	3	2	1	2	1	3	2	1
2	1	2	3	1	3	1	1	1	1
2	1	2	3	2	3	3	2	3	1
3	2	2	1	3	1	2	3	1	2

Add to 9

Teacher Directions: See page 6.

5	2	2	1	1	2	5	5	5	2
4	2	3	1	3	2	1	2	3	4
5	4	5	4	1	5	2	5	5	2
1	5	3	2	1	2	1	2	1	4
2	5	3	3	1	5	1	2	1	2
5	3	5	1	5	1	4	3	4	1
4	3	3	4	1	4	3	2	5	1
4	4	3	1	4	3	5	1	3	2
5	4	5	3	2	1	2	2	3	3
1	2	2	2	3	1	4	4	1	5

Add to 10

Teacher Directions: See page 6.

4	3	4	5	4	3	2	1	5	5
6	4	4	6	1	2	3	3	6	6
4	5	5	1	6	5	3	6	1	6
5	2	1	4	1	2	4	6	1	4
1	4	3	5	5	6	4	3	1	3
1	5	3	4	4	5	4	3	4	3
2	4	6	2	3	2	3	2	6	3
5	6	4	1	5	6	3	2	6	2
5	2	2	6	6	1	6	3	2	1
4	5	5	4	6	5	4	6	2	6

Counting Pennies and Nickels

Use different combinations of coins to make the same amount of money.
Write the number of each coin you used to make 8¢.

How many different ways can 8¢ be made?

of   pennies   +   nickels   = 8¢

1. _____ + _____ = 8¢

2. _____ + _____ = 8¢

My favorite way to make 8¢ is

(Glue coins above to make 8¢.)

Cut out the money below. Use the coins to make different solutions for the problem.

Counting Pennies, Nickels, and Dimes

Use different combinations of coins to make the same amount of money. Write the number of each coin you used to make 10¢.

How many different ways can 10¢ be made?

of   pennies   +   nickels   +   dimes   = 10¢

1. _____ + _____ + _____ = 10¢

2. _____ + _____ + _____ = 10¢

3. _____ + _____ + _____ = 10¢

4. _____ + _____ + _____ = 10¢

My favorite way to make 10¢ is

(Glue coins above to make 10¢.)

Cut out the money below. Use the coins to make different solutions for the problem.

Coin Combinations #1

Use different combinations of coins to make the same amount of money. Write the number of each coin you used to make 20¢. (Use the coins on page 70).

How many different ways can 20¢ be made?

of   pennies   +   nickels   +   dimes   = 20¢

1. _____ + _____ + _____ = 20¢

2. _____ + _____ + _____ = 20¢

3. _____ + _____ + _____ = 20¢

4. _____ + _____ + _____ = 20¢

5. _____ + _____ + _____ = 20¢

6. _____ + _____ + _____ = 20¢

7. _____ + _____ + _____ = 20¢

8. _____ + _____ + _____ = 20¢

9. _____ + _____ + _____ = 20¢

My favorite way to make 20¢ is

(Glue coins here to make 20¢.)

Coin Combinations #2

Use different combinations of coins to make the same amount of money. Write the number of each coin you used to make 28¢. (Use the coins on page 70.)

How many different ways can 28¢ be made?

# of pennies	+	nickels	+	dimes	+	quarters	= 28¢
1. _____	+	_____	+	_____	+	_____	= 28¢
2. _____	+	_____	+	_____	+	_____	= 28¢
3. _____	+	_____	+	_____	+	_____	= 28¢
4. _____	+	_____	+	_____	+	_____	= 28¢
5. _____	+	_____	+	_____	+	_____	= 28¢
6. _____	+	_____	+	_____	+	_____	= 28¢
7. _____	+	_____	+	_____	+	_____	= 28¢
8. _____	+	_____	+	_____	+	_____	= 28¢
9. _____	+	_____	+	_____	+	_____	= 28¢
10. _____	+	_____	+	_____	+	_____	= 28¢
11. _____	+	_____	+	_____	+	_____	= 28¢
12. _____	+	_____	+	_____	+	_____	= 28¢

My favorite way to make 28¢ is

(Glue coins here to make 28¢.)

Coin Manipulatives

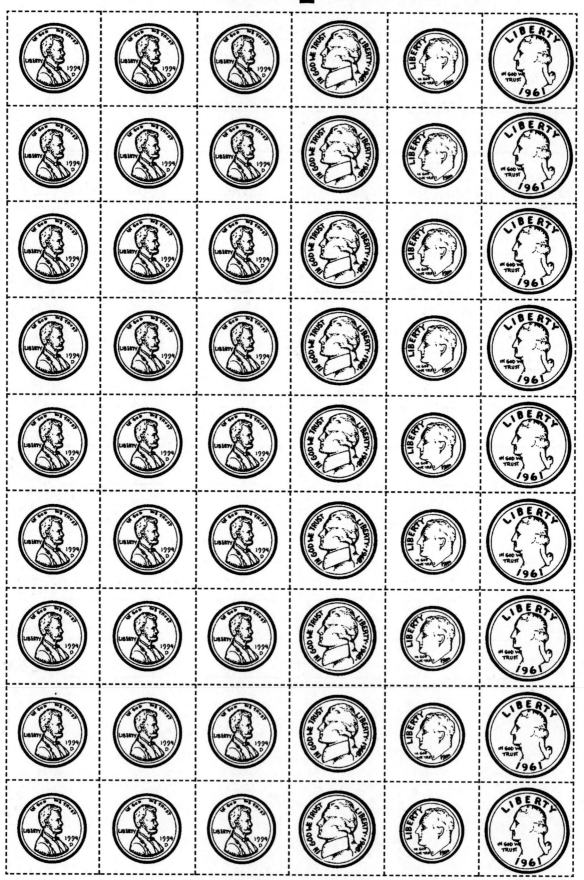

Count the Circles

How many circles are in the picture? Count them and then color the picture.

There are _____ circles.

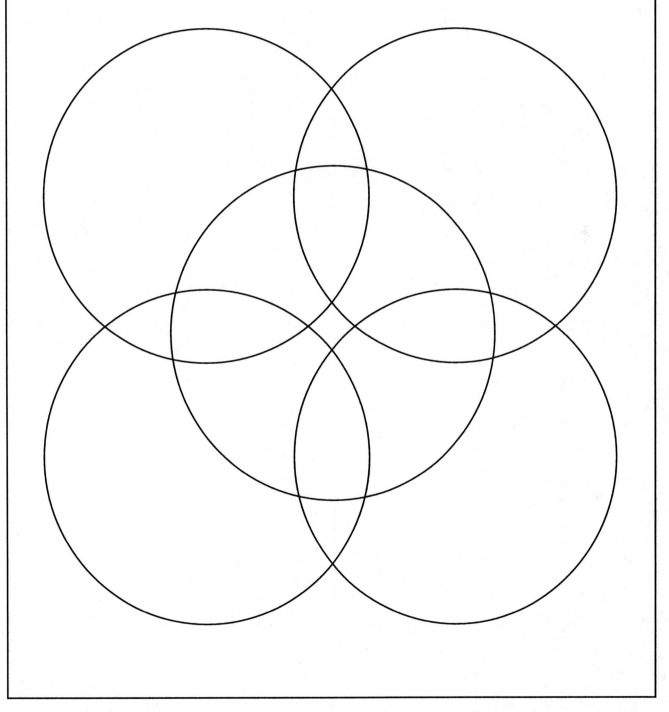

Count the Squares

How many squares are in the picture? Count them and then color the picture.

There are _____ squares.

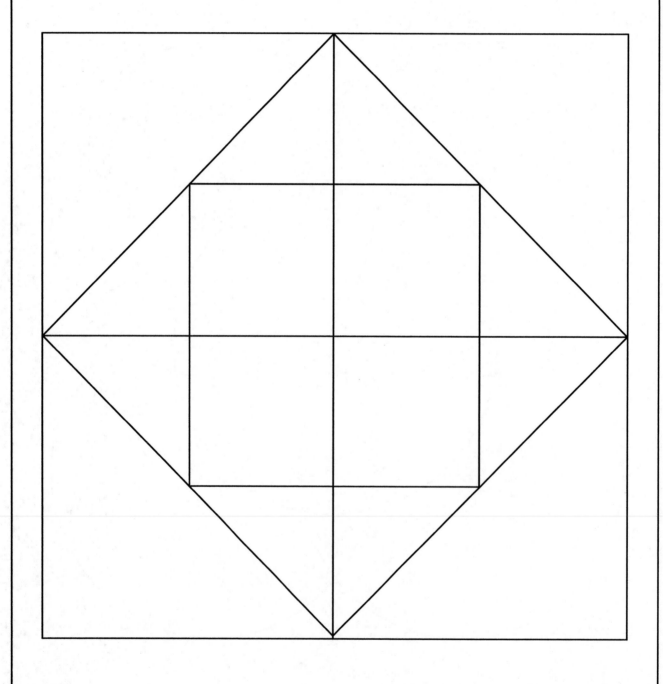

Count the Triangles

How many triangles are in the picture? Count them and then color the picture.

There are _____ triangles.

What's My Sign? #1

Fill in the missing +, −, or = sign.

1. $3 \square 2 = 5$

2. $6 - 1 \square 5$

3. $9 \square 3 = 6$

4. $2 \square 7 = 9$

5. $1 \square 3 = 4$

6. $4 + 3 \square 7$

7. $9 \square 6 = 3$

8. $6 + 2 \square 8$

9. $10 \square 5 = 15$

10. $12 \square 6 = 6$

11. $14 \square 4 = 10$

12. $7 \square 5 = 12$

What's My Sign? #2

Fill in the missing + or − signs to solve the problem.

1. $2 \square 3 \square 1 = 4$

2. $6 \square 4 \square 3 = 5$

3. $3 \square 1 \square 2 = 4$

4. $2 \square 4 \square 3 = 9$

5. $7 \square 1 \square 2 = 8$

6. $3 \square 4 \square 1 = 8$

7. $9 \square 1 \square 5 = 5$

8. $3 \square 2 \square 1 = 0$

9. $4 \square 2 \square 0 = 2$

10. $6 \square 3 \square 1 = 4$

11. $2 \square 5 \square 5 = 2$

12. $7 \square 7 \square 4 = 4$

13. $3 \square 2 \square 1 = 6$

14. $4 \square 2 \square 4 = 2$

15. $6 \square 2 \square 6 = 2$

16. $8 \square 7 \square 6 = 7$

Letters

Reproduce copies as needed. Have students cut out and use these letters to help them with some of the language arts activities.

a	b	c	d	e	f
g	h	i	j	k	l
m	n	o	p	q	r
s	t	u	v	w	x
		y	z		

Numbers

Reproduce copies as needed. Have students cut out and use these numbers to help them with some of the math activities.

1	2
3	4
5	6
7	8
9	0

Answer Key

Page 7
1. cap
2. net
3. man
4. cat
5. ice
6. leaf

Mystery word: pencil

Page 8
1. tent
2. nest
3. paddle
4. canoe
5. hamburger
6. egg
7. crab

Mystery word: teacher

Page 9
1. shell
2. scarecrow
3. flag
4. sew
5. jet
6. bear

Mystery word: eraser

Page 10
1. deer
2. bed
3. basket
4. kite

Mystery word: desk
Sentences will vary.

Page 11
1. clown
2. hat
3. band
4. bike
5. star

Mystery word: chair
Sentences will vary.

Page 12
1. dish
2. cloud
3. hen
4. octopus
5. book
6. lamp

Mystery word: school
Sentences will vary.

Page 13
1. chair
2. orange

3. cat
4. yarn
5. moon
6. sun

Mystery word: crayon
Sentences will vary.

Page 14
1. shoe
2. tree
3. umbrella
4. dime
5. fence
6. nickel
7. mat

Mystery word: student
Sentences will vary.

Page 15
1. apple
2. milk
3. bacon
4. bread
5. waffle
6. grapes
7. hay

Mystery word: library
Sentences will vary.

Page 16
1. cricket
2. moth
3. worm
4. grasshopper
5. ladybug
6. ant
7. bee
8. butterfly

Mystery word: computer
Sentences will vary.

Page 17
orange, brown, purple, yellow, green, red
Rule: All of the words are color words.
Favorite color: Answers will vary.

Page 18
jr., capt., CA, in., min., ft.
Rule: They are all abbreviations.
Other abbreviations will vary.

Page 19
checkers, Uno, chess, Yahtzee,
Monopoly, Memory
Rule: They are all board games.

Page 20
May, September, October, April,
January, July

Rule: They are all months of the year.
Sentences will vary.

Page 21
1. videotape
2. watercolor
3. overhead
4. chalkboard
5. bookcase
6. basketball
7. hopscotch
8. notebook
9. classmate
10. playground

Page 22
1. strawberry
2. milkshake
3. peanut
4. pancake
5. cupcake
6. watermelon
7. hotdog
8. popcorn
9. grapefruit
10. pineapple

Page 23
1. hummingbird
2. ladybug
3. butterfly
4. grasshopper
5. goldfish
6. hammerhead
7. seahorse
8. roadrunner
9. jellyfish
10. bulldog

Pages 24–30: Listed below are sample
words that can be made. There are
many other words that can be made
using the same letters.
Mind Challenge: Many different words
can be made.

Page 24
1. mat, am
2. and, an
3. top, to
4. map, am
5. sea, as
6. sop, so
7. tap, at

Page 25
1. our, or
2. met, me

Answer Key *(cont.)*

3. ran, an
4. top, to
5. aim, am
6. ink, in
7. sit, it

Page 26
1. fit, it
2. pin, in
3. our, or
4. ask, as
5. eat, at
6. fir, if
7. she, he

Page 27
1. spin, pin, in
2. pats, sat, at
3. hear, her, he
4. tape, tap, at
5. what, hat, at
6. tick, kit, it
7. hilt, hit, it

Page 28
1. peas, sap, as
2. slap, sap, as
3. dove, doe, do
4. over, ore, or
5. ants, ant, as
6. stir, sir, is
7. rink, ink, in

Page 29
1. rats, rat, at
2. pant, tan, at
3. open, one, on
4. rose, ore, or
5. sink, ink, in
6. weep, pew, we
7. late, tea, at

Page 30
1. later, tale, eat, at
2. diner, dine, din, in
3. pleas, peas, sea, as
4. stale, sale, sea, as
5. pleat, tale, eat, at
6. cream, cram, ram, am
7. stink, knit, tin, it

Pages 31–42: Students' own logic problems and sentences will vary.

Page 32
1. eraser, pencil, crayons
2. eraser, crayons, pencil
3. pencil, crayons, eraser
4. pencil, eraser, crayons

5. eraser, pencil, crayons
6. crayons, eraser, pencil
7. pencil, eraser, crayons
8. crayons, pencil, eraser
9. crayons, eraser, pencil
10. pencil, crayons, eraser

Page 34
1. stars, sun, moon
2. moon, sun, stars
3. sun, stars, moon
4. moon, stars, sun
5. sun, moon, stars
6. stars, moon, sun
7. sun, stars, moon
8. stars, sun, moon
9. moon, stars, sun
10. sun, moon, stars

Page 36
1. crab, octopus, fish, oyster
2. octopus, fish, crab, oyster
3. fish, crab, oyster, octopus
4. oyster, octopus, fish, crab
5. fish, crab, octopus, oyster
6. octopus, crab, oyster, fish
7. crab, oyster, fish, octopus
8. oyster, fish, octopus, crab
9. crab, fish, oyster, octopus
10. fish, octopus, crab, oyster

Page 38
1. hippo, giraffe, panda, kangaroo
2. kangaroo, hippo, giraffe, panda
3. giraffe, hippo, kangaroo, panda
4. panda, hippo, giraffe, kangaroo
5. hippo, kangaroo, panda, giraffe
6. hippo, kangaroo, panda, giraffe
7. kangaroo, panda, hippo, giraffe
8. panda, giraffe, hippo, kangaroo
9. hippo, kangaroo, giraffe, panda
10. kangaroo, hippo, panda, giraffe

Page 40
1. rolling pin, recipe card, spoon, mixing bowl, milk
2. spoon, mixing bowl, milk, rolling pin, recipe card
3. mixing bowl, recipe card, spoon, milk, rolling pin
4. milk, recipe card, mixing bowl, spoon, rolling pin
5. milk, rolling pin, recipe card, spoon, mixing bowl
6. recipe card, rolling pin, spoon, mixing bowl, milk

7. milk, recipe card, spoon, mixing bowl, rolling pin
8. rolling pin, milk, recipe card, spoon, mixing bowl
9. mixing bowl, milk, rolling pin, recipe card, spoon
10. spoon, recipe card, mixing bowl, milk, rolling pin

Page 42
1. sailboat, train, bus, car, plane
2. car, sailboat, plane, bus, train
3. plane, train, car, bus, sailboat
4. train, bus, car, plane, sailboat
5. plane, car, bus, sailboat, train
6. plane, bus, car, sailboat, train
7. train, sailboat, bus, car, plane
8. car, plane, bus, sailboat, train
9. train, car, sailboat, plane, bus
10. car, bus, plane, sailboat, train

Pages 43–46: The numbers can be arranged in a variety of ways. The solutions below are just suggestions.

Page 43
Row 1: 7, 3, 2
Row 2: 5, 1, 6
Row 3: 0, 8, 4

Page 44
Row 1: 8, 1, 6
Row 2: 3, 5, 7
Row 3: 4, 9, 2

Page 45
Row 1: 2, 9, 7
Row 2: 6, 4, 8
Row 3: 10, 5, 3

Page 46
Row 1: 9, 11, 1
Row 2: 2, 7, 12
Row 3: 10, 3, 8

Pages 47–60: Beside each clue are the numbers of the pictures that should be crossed out. Sentences will vary.

Page 47
1. 1, 2, 5, 6, 8, 9, 11
2. 3, 4, 10
3. 12
Answer: #7

Page 48
1. 2, 5, 8, 11
2. 1, 3, 10, 12
3. 6, 7, 9
Answer: #4

Answer Key *(cont.)*

Page 49
1. 1, 3, 10, 11
2. 6, 7
3. 5, 9, 12
Answer: #2

Page 50
1. 6, 8, 9
2. 1, 3, 5, 7, 10
3. 4, 11
Answer: #12

Page 51
1. 4, 9, 11
2. 1, 6, 8, 10, 11
3. 12
4. 3
5. 5
6. 7
Answer: #2

Page 52
1. 2, 3, 5, 7, 12
2. 6, 8
3. 1
4. 9, 10
5. 4
Answer: #11

Page 53
strawberries—Lee
grapes—Gus
watermelon—Vincent
Bonus: strawberry, watermelon

Page 54
fishing—Dean
canoeing—Jake
marshmallows—Reba
Bonus: Dean

Page 55
Eagles—Dan
Sharks—Ann
Tigers—Jan
Bonus: Jan

Page 56
January—Latoya
March—Cara
August—Patrick
November—Freddy
Bonus: 8 months

Page 57
hiking boots—Ralph
cowboy boots—Thomas
sandals—Maureen
tennis shoes—Emma

Bonus: cowboy boots, sandals

Page 58
Bubbles—Chelsea, white
Ranger—Sean, gray
Spot—Howie, black
Bonus: Answers will vary.

Page 59
blueberry—Noreen, 5 pieces
cherry—Belle, 6 pieces
strawberry—Cedric, 7 pieces
Bonus: Cedric

Page 60
blue—Tonya, 15 frogs
green—Gilbert, 5 frogs
orange—Chris, 10 frogs
Bonus: counting by 5's

Pages 61–65: Answers will vary.

Pages 66–69: Favorite ways will vary.

Page 66
3p 1n
8p

Page 67
5p 1n
10p
2n
1d

Page 68
20p
15p 1n
10p 2n
10p 1d
5p 3n
5p 1n 1d
4n
2n 1d
2d

Page 69
28p
23p 1n
18p 2n
18p 1d
13p 3n
13p 1n 1d
8p 4n
8p 2n 1d
8p 2d
3p 5n
3p 3n 1d
3p 1n 2d

Page 71
5 circles

Page 72
11 squares

Page 73
12 triangles

Page 74
1. +
2. =
3. −
4. +
5. +
6. =
7. −
8. =
9. +
10. −
11. −
12. +

Page 75
1. +, −
2. −, +
3. −, +
4. +, +
5. −, +
6. +, +
7. +, −
8. −, −
9. −, − or +
10. −, +
11. +, −
12. −, +
13. +, +
14. +, −
15. +, −
16. −, +